21 Ways

TO BUILD YOUR

Dental Practice

WITH A Book

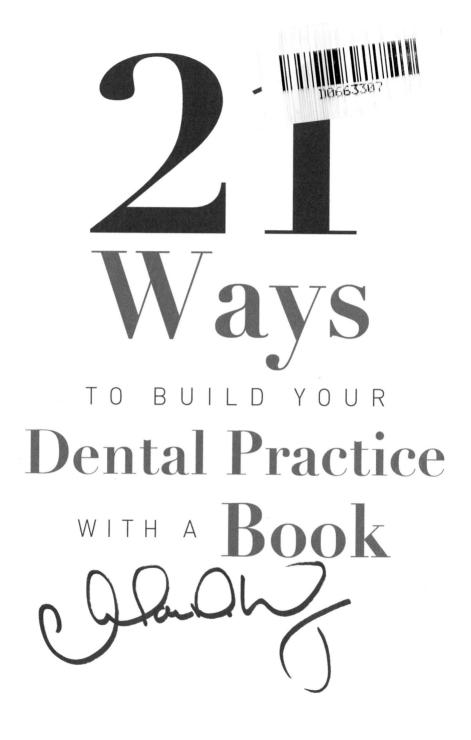

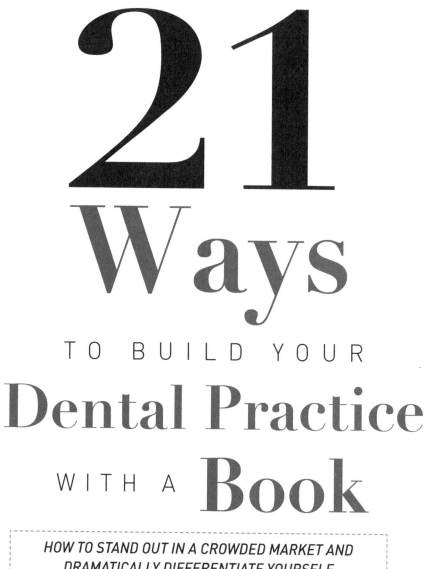

21 Ways

TO BUILD YOUR

Dental Practice

WITH A Book

HOW TO STAND OUT IN A CROWDED MARKET AND
DRAMATICALLY DIFFERENTIATE YOURSELF
AS THE AUTHORITY, CELEBRITY AND EXPERT

ADAM WITTY & MICHAEL HUH

Published by Advantage, Charleston, South Carolina.
Member of Advantage Media Group.

ADVANTAGE is a registered trademark and the Advantage colophon is a trademark of Advantage Media Group, Inc.

Printed in the United States of America.

ISBN: 978-159932-479-1
LCCN: 2013957816

This publication is designed to provide accurate and authoritative information in regard to the subject matter covered. It is sold with the understanding that the publisher is not engaged in rendering legal, accounting, or other professional services. If legal advice or other expert assistance is required, the services of a competent professional person should be sought.

Advantage Media Group is proud to be a part of the Tree Neutral® program. Tree Neutral offsets the number of trees consumed in the production and printing of this book by taking proactive steps such as planting trees in direct proportion to the number of trees used to print books. To learn more about Tree Neutral, please visit **www.treeneutral.com**. To learn more about Advantage's commitment to being a responsible steward of the environment, please visit **www.advantagefamily.com/green**

Advantage Media Group is a publisher of business, self-improvement, and professional development books and online learning. We help entrepreneurs, business leaders, and professionals share their Stories, Passion, and Knowledge to help others Learn & Grow. Do you have a manuscript or book idea that you would like us to consider for publishing? Please visit **advantagefamily.com** or call **1.866.775.1696.**

FOREWORD

DEAR PROSPECTIVE AUTHOR:

Are you intrigued by the idea of being a published author, having a book proudly displayed in your office, in bookstores and online? Can you imagine the increased credibility, marketability and prestige that will flow to you and your practice because you are a published author?

Should *you* have a book? Is it possible for you to become an author and enjoy a whole new level of authority and position as an expert in your local area? Is it possible to get your own book without the hassles of writing and publishing and spending hundreds of hours of your time? And can you still produce a book that even your harshest critics will admire, that your dental team and patients point to with pride, that gives you "bragging rights" around the Thanksgiving table and at your reunion, and that makes Mom proud? *We think you'll like our answer.*

On the other hand, in this increasingly challenging, competitive market, can you afford ***not*** to have a book and miss out on this time-tested and professional way to build your practice as nothing else can?

Will you be caught short *because your top competitor wrote the book you always wanted to write* but never got around to? Will you be kicking yourself for not acting?

The value of a book for your practice is immense and when used properly, has the power of influencing your patients to say yes to your best treatment recommendations. It also has the power to *attract the exact patients you want* in your practice—the ones who value your services, accept care and show their appreciation.

Your book can give you a bulletproof marketing advantage, an edge that lasts for years and years. Once done, you can reuse it many, many times over.

Over the years, we have personally helped hundreds of dentists and medical professionals write, publish, monetize and market a book to grow their practice.

In the pages ahead you will learn what the top dentists know and, quite frankly, are happy to keep secret: how to market and grow a dental practice with a book.

Enjoy the read ahead!

ADAM D. WITTY
FOUNDER & CHIEF EXECUTIVE OFFICER
ADVANTAGE MEDIA GROUP

P.S. I've included stories of successful authors' use of their books throughout this work so you can see outside the box normally associated with dentistry.

Why is that important to you?

Here is a huge hint: Some of the greatest business transformations of all time have occurred with ideas borrowed from *other businesses outside the primary one. Borrowed revolutionary concepts* and *ideas have created entire industries.* Henry Ford became the wealthiest man on earth by borrowing an idea from a Chicago meatpacking plant. A packaged foods manufacturer changed its entire system of manufacturing by copying the pit crews at an Indy race, generating an additional three hundred million dollars in profits in one year.

May one of the ideas contained in this book be the **spark** that **changes *your* practice.**

AS A DENTIST, DO YOU REALLY NEED A BOOK?

As a dentist, you practice in the geographical area from which most of your patients come. Why is a book a good idea for you? You aren't going to be getting most of your patients from a national base, so you don't really have any use for a book. Right? Wrongola. That is how the average dentist thinks.

Think counter intuitively with us for a moment. You, above all, don't want to be average, getting average fees, delivering average services, settling for average success, living the life you don't want, do you?

You see, it isn't necessary for your book to be a big national best seller for it to have a *profound, positive impact* on you and your practice. Local is entirely okay!

Because you are only slightly famous, where you live can be enough to completely transform your practice into the one you always dreamed about. A book can make you a big fish in a big pond or make you the dominant fish in a small pond. Either way, you win. This book will help you see why this is true. Once you have listened to the words rolling around in your head, consider them carefully. We believe that your gut will guide you to your right answer and for many the answer will be: "Yes, I need a book," if not now, then maybe sometime in your future. But you need not wait, because we can make the work of creating a book as simple as saying yes, and you have hardly lifted a finger.

Prepare to get excited. I certainly was as I wrote this book. You are going to learn a thing or two. Let's get started.

TABLE OF CONTENTS

REGISTER YOUR BOOK

AND ACCESS FREE RESOURCES FOR POTENTIAL AUTHORS!

It doesn't matter where you are in the world, Adam can help you share your Stories, Passion, and Knowledge with the world in the form of a published book.

Visit BUILDYOURDENTALPRACTICE.COM/REGISTER to access these free resources:

 RECEIVE a subscription to the Author Success University™ monthly teleseminar wherein successful authors and book marketing experts reveal their tips and tricks for marketing and growing a business with a book

 REGISTER for a webinar led by Adam Witty: "How to Quickly Write, Publish, And Profit From A Book That Will Grow Your Business"

 COMPLETE Advantage's Publishing Questionnaire and receive a complimentary Discovery Call with an acquisitions editor to help you determine if your ideas, concepts, or manuscript are worth turning into a book

ACCESS ALL OF THE ABOVE FREE RESOURCES BY REGISTERING YOUR BOOK AT
BUILDYOURDENTALPRACTICE.COM/REGISTER

21 Ways

How a Book Makes You the Authority, Celebrity, and Expert in Your Market

By Adam Witty

How a Book Makes You the Authority, Celebrity, and Expert in Your Market

BY ADAM WITTY

Have you ever heard of Robert Kiyosaki, author of *Rich Dad Poor Dad*? Robert has gone on to make a fortune in speaking, coaching, training and, of course, his business and real estate interests. That said, it was Robert's book that made him famous. It was that book that made him the credible, "go-to" expert.

How about Tim Ferris of *The 4 Hour Work Week*? Have you ever heard of him? Prior to his book, no one had a clue who Tim Ferris was. **The book made him famous; the book has made him credible**, and Tim has wisely used the book to his full advantage by making appearances with highly paid speaking fees and getting top publicity on television, radio and in print.

Both of these authors would be classified as celebrities. They have come to dominate their respective fields as experts and gurus. What bestowed this "guru" status upon them? You got it—a book!

Have you ever considered the word *authority*? **What do the first six letters spell?** *Author.* **Consumers naturally see authors as authorities and experts on the subject of their book. After all, if they were not experts, how could they have possibly written books?**

As a dentist or medical professional, you will naturally attract more patients to your practice if you are seen as the expert and authority. People want to be a patient of "the famous dentist." People will brag about you to their friends at cocktail parties. Everyone likes to know someone famous. Being the author of a book makes you famous, credible and an authority and expert—right where you live.

BE THE CELEBRITY PROSPECTS CHOOSE FIRST: WHY ANY PROFESSIONAL WHO WANTS TO STAND OUT NEEDS A BOOK

Why is it that some professionals and businesses do so well, while others struggle for success? And why do some businesses outsell and outcompete others, even when all factors seem to be equal? If you've ever wondered how to stand out in a crowded, competitive marketplace, you need to consider the example of author, business coach, and dentist, Dr. Charles Martin.

As the founder and CEO of Richmond Smile Center, Dr. Martin could be like many dentists across the country:

working hard for success and doing reasonably well. But Dr. Martin is also the author of three books, and because of this, his story is far different.

As a published author, he has gained an instant advantage over his competition. As Dr. Martin notes, "The great advantage of being a published author is it gives you a status point that most of your competitors do not have."

In part, this status occurs because people view authors as experts in their respective fields. However, books also provide a great way to *attract* people to your practice or business. This is far better than trying to hunt for them in a crowded marketplace. "A book is about 'pull marketing,'" says Dr. Martin. "It's about how people can discover you and hear what you have to say. You actually start to create a relationship unilaterally."

By featuring a book in his marketing, Dr. Martin believes it gives him "more presence and prominence in the mind of the person you want to be your customer, client, or patient." Plus, books work, even if your prospect *doesn't* read it.

"If you have someone actually read your book, it's a golden ticket. And I say *golden* ticket because if they read your book and like what you have to say, you've got a client, customer, or patient right there. If they don't read it, the fact that you've taken the time, energy, and effort to write a book gives you all sorts of presence and position in the mind of your prospective client, patient, or customer."

Either way, it's a win for any business owner because a book makes you famous *where it's most important.* "You need to be famous or at least well known where you live because if you have a brick-and-mortar business, that's where your clients are mostly coming from."

HOW AUTHORS CREATE FAME IN THEIR TARGET MARKETS

In addition to creating a prominent local presence, a book provides another advantage, especially for professionals. "Generally, most professionals are restricted on what they can say or do in their advertising and marketing," explains Dr. Martin. "So, a book gives you another way to get your message out and do it without infringing on those regulations."

Plus there's an added bonus: "By marketing your book directly, it's an easy pathway for your prospective patient to get to know you, understand what you think, and agree with what you have to say."

And when it comes to marketing a book, there are several ways to do it. One of the easiest things Dr. Martin does is display his books in waiting and consultation rooms. His books are also prominently featured on his website.

He also uses radio ads to successfully market his book by inviting listeners to get a free copy. The book allows them to get to know Dr. Martin. It also reinforces that he is trying to help rather than just sell.

If you're unsure whether to start with radio, he advises that any business owner can begin with print advertising. "You can even use classified ads. You'd be amazed at how little you pay for a classified ad, particularly when you cover a wide region." Dr. Martin also suggests book-signing events. "You can have a book signing in your practice or business. It gives you an excuse to gather people and hold a client or patient appreciation event."

Yet the list doesn't end here. Increased referrals are another very profitable outcome of a book. "There's nothing better than to give your clients or patients a couple copies of your book to hand out to anyone who may need what you do." He even gives copies to vendors and suppliers because "you never know who they might refer. When they can say, 'My dentist has published a book or books,' it gives them a little emotional ammunition to speak up when someone they know needs your services."

Another way to take full advantage of your book is to include it in a "shock and awe" or "trust box." This marketing tool is essentially a package that usually includes

- A welcome letter
- A list of client reviews or testimonials
- Small gifts
- Patient questionnaires and information forms
- A CD or DVD
- And, of course, a book

All of this is then mailed to a prospective client "to provide an overwhelming amount of evidence and proof that you're the right selection for them," or to a new client "to reaffirm their decision to choose you."

YET BOOKS GO FAR BEYOND MARKETING OPPORTUNITIES

Dr. Martin also uses his books to support and promote new business ventures, such as speaking and consulting.

"As a writer, speaker, and practicing dentist, when I share a book with a speakers bureau or a dental manufacturing company, they all say 'Okay, this guy's got a book and it's written well.' So, it's almost a sample of my work or what I'll say. It gives you a leg up on the competition."

He also uses his books to support speaking engagements. "I give my books to the attendees of my dental implant or cosmetic seminars because it's part of the entire trust equation. Books build trust. Simple as can be."

And his business ventures include more than seminars. "My books helped me to get a consulting job with a big dental manufacturing company. And it was very lucrative."

All of these marketing and new business opportunities have certainly increased his income. "For what it costs you to have a book versus the benefits, it's at least a ten to one, and I would say more like a twenty to one, differential."

YET THERE ARE MANY OTHER WAYS THAT AUTHORSHIP BENEFITS HIS PRACTICE

For one thing, his book provides patients with information they need on dental conditions and beneficial procedures. This information is often the tipping point to move them forward with helpful treatments.

"As dentists, we actually have to be able to answer their questions as succinctly as possible, yet, display our expertise. A book is one of the key ways to do this." And to help patients along, Dr. Martin takes one extra step. "I take a book and mark which pages to read. The fact of the matter is that few people are going to read your entire book, but things they do read can be a big deal."

However, his books help more than patients. They are also important training and recruiting tools, which is why he gives copies to all staff. "A book can certainly be used to help train your existing staff on how you think or on how your business works." And benefits go well beyond training. "There's no end to what you can do but it's amazing what it does for your team to be part of a group when the leader or founder has a book or books."

Books also help him to recruit top-notch staff. For one thing, "it helps you to understand who's really serious about a position because if they're really determined, they'll go to your website. They'll look around and they'll look for what you've written."

And he believes that authors stand a better chance of recruiting staff that are a good fit. By describing who you are, what you stand for, and what your values are, you're more likely to find a person you enjoy working with.

In addition to attracting staff you like to work with, books help you to automatically reel in your ideal clients, as well.

"There's hardly a better method to express who you are, what you think, how you think and why, related to your services and products. With a book, you are taking a position. And by taking a position, you get the people who like you coming towards you, while people who don't like you, move away."

Of course, this makes your business far more enjoyable. But there is another benefit. "You also filter who comes to you so that person comes in smiling, liking you, and being predisposed to saying yes to your offerings from the get-go." This reason is why so many authors find it easier to raise fees in addition to attracting new patients or clients.

And Dr. Martin points out yet another bonus: "You have the ability to promote the very things that you want to do, that give you the most satisfaction or create your best business." In other words, you can become a celebrity in the specialties *you enjoy most* and attract clients or patients who want these services.

"I WOULDN'T WANT TO PRACTICE WITHOUT A BOOK."

After reading the above, it's pretty easy to see why Dr. Martin would make this statement today. And it's why he recommends that all professionals write a book, even if they feel they have nothing to say. "The reality is, if you're an expert, you have a whole lot to say that you probably haven't thought about. You have information that someone who is not an expert wants to know!"

The benefits of being a published author are many, but when it comes to your business, a book is a game changer. "It certainly stacks the odds in your favor when you're trying to move someone from 'thinking about it' to a 'yes.' If you don't have a book, you are taking chances you shouldn't have to take."

It's probably no surprise that Dr. Martin is the author of three books, and has two more in the works. And he walks the talk when it comes to using books to build his business. "A book fits into everything. It fits into your internal systems and your external systems. It fits into your offline or direct mail systems. It fits into your online systems. And it helps referrals. It helps you get publicity. There's virtually no place where it doesn't have an effect."

And while increased business and income is often the goal for writing a book, Dr. Martin reminds us that deeper benefits exist. "Not only is there a return on investment financially, there's a return on investment emotionally and professionally from the admiration and respect you get from the people you serve."

Is there any better reason to get started on writing your book right now? At Advantage Media Group we help professionals write and publish books that make their businesses easier, more enjoyable, and far more profitable. Contact us today for your free consultation. We'll answer your questions and tell you how easy the publishing process can be. Secure your private appointment now by visiting advantagefamily.com/dental or by calling 1.866.775.1696.

21 Ways

Become a Darling
of the Media

Get Your Fair Share of Media Coverage
and Free Publicity with a Book

BY MICHAEL HUH

Become a Darling of the Media

Get Your Fair Share of Media Coverage and Free Publicity with a Book

BY MICHAEL HUH

Many dentists daydream about being featured as speakers at the biggest industry conventions and even as guest experts on television and radio. At the very least, these same dentists want to be highlighted in their industry trade journals and publications. For most, all of the above remains just a dream. Why? Most folks don't realize "it isn't about them." The media doesn't care about you; they only care about delivering good content to their readers/viewers/listeners. **They want a great story. A book can be a great story.**

Sending press releases and hoping for coverage just doesn't cut it anymore. **You have to give the media something to talk about. A book is something to talk about.** Reporters are looking for sources for their stories and interviews each and every day. In fact, radio alone interviews over 10,000 people every single day. *Why aren't they interviewing you?* You haven't given them a reason.

Being an author makes you an expert. It also makes you credible. Reporters love interviewing credible experts for their stories, whether it's radio, TV, print, or online.

I want to tell you about Advantage author Jim Ziegler. Jim's main business is serving as a consultant to automobile dealers. In fact, Jim was recently the keynote speaker at the National Automotive Dealer Association conference. Perhaps more notably, Jim has been a monthly columnist in industry-revered *Dealer Magazine* since October 1998 (the same year Jim released his book). Who do you think reads *Dealer Magazine*? Ding, ding, ding—you guessed correctly —owners of automobile dealerships, the same people who hire Jim. By the way, Jim was an absolute unknown to *Dealer Magazine* until he mailed them a review copy of his book. The book ignited the spark that lead to his monthly column in the magazine.

Would you like to be writing a monthly article for a large publication? Don't you think it would be a lot easier for you to get business if you were a columnist in your industry's largest trade journal?

As Jim will be the first to tell you, outside auto, nobody knows who he is. But inside the auto industry, Jim is a rock star. In fact, the president of Ford Motor Co. flew him up to

Detroit in the company's corporate jet to consult with them. **Would you like to be a rock star within your industry?** Would you like to consult for the largest company in your industry—and fly in their corporate jet, to boot?

As a dentist, this could translate into writing a local column for the newspaper. As the author, you will be regarded as a valued source and expert to comment on local and national stories on oral health and dentistry in general by your local media.

A book could very well translate into national publicity, leading to your being interviewed on national television stations such as CNN or FOX News or for articles in *USA Today* or *Newsweek*. You could become the resident expert to speak on national issues relating to dentistry. What most dentists don't know is that these media outlets are always looking for experts who can comment and give information and guidance.

If you are interested in speaking to your profession, your book could be the entrée to the list of speakers requested to present at major dental conferences, or the beginnings of a featured article or monthly column in a dental trade journal. The possibilities are limited only by your imagination.

21 Ways

Use a Book for Patient Gifts and to Create Patient Loyalty

By Adam Witty

Use a Book for Patient Gifts and to Create Patient Loyalty

BY ADAM WITTY

Are you looking for the perfect gift for your best patients? Look no further, the perfect present has arrived!

THE MOST PROFITABLE COMPANIES AROUND THE WORLD BOAST THE MOST FANATICAL AND LOYAL CLIENTS AND CUSTOMERS.

There is a direct correlation between fanatical clients and profit. These companies have a plan to regularly show appreciation to their clients. I want you to think about all of the companies that have sent you gifts of appreciation for your business. That thought is over pretty quickly, is it not? Few businesses do this. Few practices ever shower their patients with appreciation, providing ever more reason as to why you should be sending patient gifts.

Have you heard of the Pareto principle? Perhaps you are familiar with the 80/20 rule? It is the rule of the vital few. Made famous by Italian economist Vilfredo Pareto, the rule states that **80 percent of effects come from 20 percent of causes**. Using that rule, we oftentimes find that 80 percent of tax dollars are paid by 20 percent of the tax-paying population. Or that the top 20 percent of our patients make up 80 percent of our profit. Look around, you will find the Pareto principle to be true in most all aspects of your life.

With that said, **what are you currently doing to thank your best patients?** What are you doing to show your appreciation to that top 20 percent who are contributing 80 percent to your bottom line? Do you know the lifetime value of your patients? Most dentists do not.

Savvy dentists have a set system in place to continually thank and show appreciation to their best patients. At Advantage, we classify our publishing clients based upon a number of factors. We have elaborate systems and sequences in place for each classification. For example, a Platinum client might receive eight presents and thank-you gifts from us every year. A Gold client might receive six, and so on down the line.

Naturally, that begs the question: what do I give? How about a copy of your hot-off-the-presses book? **Books are fabulous patient gifts that double as patient retention**

tools at the same time. A book is a tool to create patient glue and stickiness. Not only does the book communicate thoughtfulness on your end, it also provides a perfectly scripted message to your patients. What you say and how you say it matters. Your book can be the near-perfect way to get your message across.

HOW TO EASILY ACHIEVE MORE EVEN AFTER YOU'VE REACHED SUCCESS: BY SHARING HIS STORIES, A SUCCESSFUL ENTREPRENEUR NETS SURPRISING RETURNS

To say that Dr. Michael Fling has achieved success is probably an understatement. In addition to his flourishing dental practice in Oklahoma City, Dr. Fling maintains a busy schedule as an advanced clinical instructor and motivational speaker.

So, when audience members asked him to share his stories in a book, he didn't hesitate. He published *32 Laps: Tipping Points That Motivate Change and Identify Meaning in Your Business and Your Life* in January 2013.

"It allows me to tie in dentistry with my philosophies. Plus, it adds credibility to what I already do." The result is another accomplishment in an already successful career. And today, he uses his book for both his speaking business and dental practice.

Dr. Fling will either sell his book or give it away, depending on the circumstances. "When I speak, I'll always have books that people can buy. Sometimes, I'll just give them copies. Last year, I did a seminar for 500 dentists and we gave books to all of them."

MOTIVATING A WIDE AUDIENCE

He believes his philosophy inspires other dentists. "In my motivational speaking, treating teeth is just part of what we (as dentists) do. What we really do is build relationships and try to find ways to make people better and to help them grow. That's more important than dentistry alone."

However, because his message reaches across boundaries, his audience also includes patients, other professionals, and even high-school students. "There are some really good messages in the book that are very meaningful to kids. I've done presentations in high schools and my children have been to some of my seminars. I love for them to go and listen to my message."

This, perhaps, is one of the deeper benefits of becoming a published author: the knowledge that you are making an impact. "To me, the book is for giving some insight to grow and be better. Whether I'm speaking to hundreds of dentists or dealing with my patients in my practice, that's the benefit of my book."

And based on comments he has received, his readers agree. "I literally had one patient say, 'I keep your book on my nightstand beside my bed. I read it over and over because it means so much to me.'"

It's comments like this that lead Dr. Fling to believe his relationships with patients have developed further since he became a published author. "It seems like my relationship with my patients and my staff just continues to grow and get stronger. The book both reinforces and enhances my relationships."

Dr. Fling will be the first to say a book is a great way to enrich an already successful career, or as he says, "to add one more arrow in the quiver." This is why he encourages everyone to write a book. "If you feel you have a message or a story to tell, just get on with it, because life is short."

And with the help of Advantage Media Group, he was able to publish his book with ease. "I'd never written a book before, so I didn't know the first thing about publishing. But they were a helpful group, so we got it done."

The helpful group at Advantage includes experienced book editors, strategists and marketers. With their input and assistance you can write a book that both shares your message and builds your business. If you'd like to become an author, visit advantagefamily.com/dental or call us at 1.866.775.1696. We'll tell you how we can help by making the process easy for you.

21 Ways

A Book Is Your Marketplace Differentiator

By Michael Huh

A Book Is Your Marketplace Differentiator

BY MICHAEL HUH

While there are over six billion people in the world, there are only about three million authors. For those who were not math majors, **being a published author makes you part of the top 0.05 percent**. How is that for differentiation?

As a dentist, **a continuing challenge is countering the thought that a dentist is a dentist is a dentist**. In other words, you are considered a commodity. Commodities are bought based on price. Ugh! This thinking forces you to charge fees like a commodity and accept less than you are worth, and it destroys your profits. Doesn't it make sense to stop playing this losing game?

Being an author instantly makes you an expert. Being an author instantly catapults you out of the "rest of the

pack." As an author, you are no longer a "me too." As an author, your credibility among patients and competitors soars. Stand out in a crowd and keep the competition back over your shoulder. Do you know where your competition stands today? Exceeding your patients' expectations only takes a little bit of effort, but *it can do a lot for your profits.* Odds say your competitors aren't publishing a book (yet).

So that begs the question: **What are you doing so differently that people will choose you over your competition?** Consumers are no longer settling for average service or the best price. They have too many choices. The patients you want are those for whom your expert status is more important than your fees. They are looking for competence. And in our society authors are considered experts with the competence to deliver the results that your best patients want. Wouldn't it make sense to be known as the authority in your area?

Being different will position you to exceed your patients' expectations. **Being an author means you have gone the extra mile.** It will pay off for you time and time again. Your patients will feel good about spending their money with you over and over again. That extra mile taken to be an author just might be the tipping point for patients to choose you.

21 Ways

Use a Book to Generate Quality Referrals

By Adam Witty

Use a Book to Generate Quality Referrals

BY ADAM WITTY

HOW MANY OF YOUR NEW PATIENTS COME FROM REFERRALS?

What percent of your existing patients provide referrals? I bet you don't know the answer. As a rule of thumb, studies show that roughly 20 percent of your patients will freely give referrals without being asked. Another 20 percent will not give referrals at all. That leaves 60 percent of your clients who probably would refer your business if you would only ask.

The most profitable businesses report that well over **70 percent of new clients come from referrals.** With the cost of advertising and marketing continuing to rise while producing lackluster results, **referrals are your best and most cost-effective marketing tool.**

Smart doctors provide books to their best patients while asking those same patients to pass the books along to friends, family and business associates that might benefit by reading their information.

The book instantly creates a "conversation starter" for your patients to give to their friends. In essence, you have greased the skids, making it easier for your patients to give you referrals. One of your most important jobs to build your practice is **making it easier for your patients to refer business to you.**

The second slam-dunk of a book is that it allows you to control the message your patients tell their referrals, guaranteeing they will say exactly what you want.

Have you ever cringed at the sound of a patient describing your practice to their referral? Just because patients do business with you does not guarantee they can deliver your "30-second commercial" correctly. In fact, your best patients may be driving new patients away by saying all the wrong things—unintentionally. Your book is a scripted masterpiece, the same masterpiece your referrals will be reading.

Give copies of your book to your best patients and then simply have them pass those books along to friends, family and colleagues who may be a fit for your practice. Doing this ensures that you control 100 percent of your message, leaving nothing to chance.

21 Ways

How to Use a Book as the Ultimate Practice Builder

By Michael Huh

How to Use a Book as the Ultimate Practice Builder

By Michael Huh

Books have been held in reverence by the cultures of the world for hundreds of years. They are the oldest and most respected of all forms of communication. Even in today's digital world, books downloaded electronically carry much of the same impact.

Authors are considered authorities because it is an arduous task to write a book (not with us); it takes a lot of time, effort, energy and "smarts" and, even then, you might not get published. (Again, not with us!)

This perception of authors means that a book is held in higher regard than other means of written communication. As such, the minds of readers are more open to the messages of books. Less filtering occurs and acceptance of "the truth of a book" is elevated far above advertising, which the public generally considers unreliable.

This attitude, rooted in our culture, thrives in the form of "real experts write books." Hmmmm. Doesn't this sound like a position you would like to enjoy without all the heavy lifting?

Now here is the even bigger secret for your practice: A book can influence your patients and prospective patients unlike any other form of communication. Its power comes from the near-instantaneous acceptance of its message by the minds and hearts of its readers. Further, even if your patients or prospective patients never read your book, you are still awarded a position of authority. You are *the* expert with the competence they want. I call this the author's effect.

The author's effect sweeps concerns, objections and hesitations aside. Authors are given this power because society has discovered, historically, that authors are trusted sources of information. Readers use your book as a sort of shortcut to locating the expert they want to take care of their needs. Recommendations of esteemed experts (authors) are often accepted without the mental gyrations that the simple expert (i.e., relatively unknown dentist) must endure.

When you are making treatment recommendations, the "I want to think about it" melts away to become "When can we get started?" The hesitation of "I am not sure" is swept away to become "Let's go ahead." The "no" that would have happened if you had not written a book becomes a resounding "yes"—from a far more enthusiastic referral source.

Moreover, a book has the power to answer the prospective patient's questions—"Who is good?" "Who should I trust with my care?"—virtually instantaneously. "He wrote the book" rockets the author to the top rung of the ladder, the top position. And if you are the first to write a book, you'll enjoy this top positioning for years to come. If you aren't the first in your area to write a book, you need a book to counter your competitor's advantage. (We can discuss how this is done so that your book becomes the preeminent one in your area with our proprietary system).

WHY SHARING YOUR PHILOSOPHY LEADS TO INCREASED INCOME: EDUCATING PATIENTS WITH A BOOK LEADS TO AN EASIER AND MORE PROFITABLE DENTAL PRACTICE

As a holistic dentist, Dr. Namrita Singh knew she needed to do more to educate her patients. "I do things differently than a lot of dentists. There isn't a whole lot of information, so I wanted to put it all together and give it to my patients. This way, they would understand where I am coming from and why I'm doing certain procedures. They would understand what my philosophy for practicing dentistry is."

So, Dr. Singh published her book, *Whole Health Dentistry: Why the Mouth Is Key to Your Body's Health,* in May 2013.

"My book definitely helps patients understand why I want them to do certain procedures. It helps them to do more for themselves and that has helped me too of course. I can provide them with the care they actually need because people no longer doubt or question what I recommend. It's a win-win situation for both of us."

Dr. Singh's book has certainly achieved her goal of education. Yet, not surprisingly, she has also created a more profitable and enjoyable practice.

"EASY MARKETING" YIELDS BIG RESULTS

Since her goal was to educate, Dr. Singh has only done "a little marketing" for her book so far. Even so, her results have been impressive.

She began by including her book in every aspect of her practice, starting with her website. Anyone who visits her site can buy a hard copy on Amazon or download it for Kindle. She also keeps copies in her waiting and patient consultation rooms. Posters in the reception area promote the book as well.

She encourages everyone to read and share the book. Not surprisingly, this tactic has resulted in new patients. "My patients will pick my book up and then give it to their friends. I have people that come in after reading a book that they got from someone else."

In addition, Dr. Singh gives copies to the specialists she refers patients to. She has noticed referrals from the specialists, in return. "They can give my book to their patients when they have questions or when they want to refer them to a general dentist."

Finally, she provides a copy to every employee, new and old. While this may not sound like a marketing strategy, she feels it improves the patient experience, which in turn helps with patient retention. "Now, my employees all have better answers for the questions my patients frequently ask. To me, my book is literally like an employee training manual."

All of these strategies were relatively easy to do. Yet the return is beyond Dr. Singh's expectations. She believes her credibility has increased along with her patients' trust. "When patients walk in to sit in my chair, they listen to me differently now. I have an easier time explaining things to them. They are more apt to listen to my explanations and do what I want them to do, whereas before, I would struggle with trying to explain why a particular thing had to be done even though it was more expensive."

Of course, her practice is easier and more enjoyable when patients are willing to do what she recommends. Plus, she no longer has to provide long, drawn-out explanations to her patients, so she saves time.

More importantly, patients are now more willing to invest in expensive procedures to protect their teeth, something fewer were willing to do before reading her book. All of this adds up to increased income.

"I felt if my patients were more educated, I would increase my income, which I did. My book has also helped me to do it in an easier fashion. So, I got more than what I wanted with my book."

With results like these, it's no wonder that Dr. Singh recommends that every professional should become an author. And thanks to Advantage Media Group's *Talk Your Book*™ program, it is easier to do than you may think. "The whole process of sitting down and writing your book is taken away. So, it's easy to get your chance to show or tell people your point of view."

She also has high praise for Advantage's staff. "They were wonderful. They were really helpful. I couldn't have done it without their help. I love being a published author. It was always a dream for me. Now, it is a dream come true."

If you dream of becoming an author, contact Advantage Media Group today. Our friendly staff will answer your questions and explain how easy it can be to talk your way through your book instead of writing it. Just visit advantagefamily.com/dental or call us at 1.866.775.1696.

21 Ways

Be a Patient Magnet

Use a Book for Lead Generation

BY ADAM WITTY

Be a Patient Magnet

Use a Book for Lead Generation

BY ADAM WITTY

Many individuals and businesses use a book to generate new leads. Rather than using the "same as the other guy" ads, they use a book to generate only the most qualified leads.

Would you like to give a book to all of your patients and best prospects that would immediately point them right back to doing business with you? That book is YOUR book. Allow me to illustrate with an example. Carl Sewell is the CEO of Sewell Automobile Companies in Dallas, Texas. In 1990 Carl penned a book titled *Customers for Life*. In the book, Carl describes in detail his company's ten commandments of customer service. Any prospect who walks into a Sewell automobile dealership receives a complimentary copy of the book, even if they were just looking. Well, as you can imagine, many of those prospects read (or at least skim) the book and learn of Carl's ten commandments of customer service. After reading the book, they realize they won't get better service anywhere else and purchase their vehicle from Sewell.

Interestingly, in 1990, when Sewell published the book, he had three dealerships in Dallas. Today, Sewell has 17 dealerships spread throughout Dallas, Fort Worth, San Antonio, Grapevine, and Plano. *Do you think the book had anything to do with that success?*

HOW CAN YOU LEVERAGE YOUR BOOK TO ACQUIRE NEW PATIENTS?

1. First, hold a client appreciation party, and provide a complimentary copy of your book as a parting gift.

2. Second, personally deliver or mail a copy of your book to all of your best prospects.

3. Finally, give a copy of your book to every potential patient who enters your doors.

Use a Book to Create Multiplicity

By Michael Huh

Use a Book to Create Multiplicity

By Michael Huh

Too much to do and not enough time to do it! This seems to be the mantra by which we live these days. We would guess that this same phrase might apply to your life too.

As dentists, you are constantly pulled in many directions, needing to be in many places at one time.

A book allows you to be in multiple places at once— figuratively, that is. But think for a minute about the power of multiplicity and leverage. Mass media is leverage. Rather than speaking to people one by one, you can, with radio and television, literally speak to millions of people at one time. A book allows you to do the same thing.

The difference between being a millionaire and multi-millionaire is nothing more than the ***power of leverage***. As the old saying goes, "the first million is always the hardest."

So why do some people plateau after making the first million while others turn the first million into 5, 10, or 20 million? The answer is leverage.

Leverage is utilizing the strengths of people, processes, media, and economies of scale to do a lot more in much less time. Leverage helps you get the most out of yourself, because you free up your time to work on the activities that are most valuable to you.

Most dentists and entrepreneurs agree that to get ahead you must work hard and work smart. **Publishing a book allows you to leverage your time by communicating with many people at once.** While writing the book might involve some heavy lifting at first (we can lighten the load a lot), it will pay dividends for the rest of your career.

Carl Sewell, mentioned earlier, has used his book for that last 20 years to grow his automobile company from one dealership to 17 dealerships. Jim Ziegler, also mentioned previously, reported that many of the top executives of the major automobile manufacturers across the globe have a copy of his book on their bookshelves. **How would you like a copy of your book to be on CEOs' coffee tables or bookshelves?**

If you want to take your practice to the next level, you need to work smart, not just hard. Multiply and leverage yourself through the power of a book.

A Book Is a Cost-Effective Marketing Tool

By Adam Witty

A Book Is a Cost-Effective Marketing Tool

BY ADAM WITTY

A book is the most powerful marketing tool in a dentist's marketing and publicity arsenal and oftentimes the most cost-effective.

WHAT IS YOUR COST PER LEAD? WHAT IS YOUR COST PER PATIENT?

These can be scary questions to answer. Most dentists would prefer not knowing, as the answers will reveal a large hole in their "marketing budget." Unless you ruthlessly track and manage your return on marketing investment you will constantly underperform.

Big, "dumb" companies routinely spend $100,000+ dollars to take out full-page "image" advertisements in national magazines and newspapers. While these ads may look good to the naked eye, they rarely do anything to move the sales needle forward. Big companies can afford to make these mistakes. Small, lean, entrepreneurial organizations cannot. Nor can a personal service business like a dental practice.

Your book is an image advertisement, business card, direct-response advertisement, and credibility builder all in one. Best of all, for less than about $5 per unit, your book can do a lot of heavy lifting. Some of this lifting is helping people understand what you offer. Do you sell a technical or complex product or service? Of course, you do. The public has very little knowledge of dentistry and its effects on their lives. They need to know enough to appreciate these effects and value them differently than they did in the past. **A book is a phenomenal tool to explain the technicalities of your dental services.**

CHAPTER 10

21 Ways

How to Be Heard Above the Noise with a Book

By Michael Huh

How to Be Heard Above the Noise with a Book

By Michael Huh

Americans are overloaded with information from e-mail, 500 channels of TV, blogs, newspapers, radio, billboards and online. To get away from the complete bombardment of information, people find and enjoy peace and quiet in reading. Where do you and others like to read? Is it on the couch next to the fire, on airplanes, in bed, on the beach, away from the spouse, kids, and coworkers?

IT IS DURING THIS ALONE TIME THAT THE READER IS CONCENTRATING ON YOU, THE AUTHOR, SOLELY.

With the average American being exposed to over 3,000 unique marketing messages daily, having a quiet sanctuary with your prospective patient or existing patient, all to yourself, is nearly impossible.

Close your eyes and picture your best patient sitting in business class on a JFK to LAX flight, reading your book. For the 4+ hours of flight, you have this person all to yourself. **You control the dialogue, conversation and message.** *Buying this time would be impossible.*

Communication is key, and without the distractions of daily "noise," books are the ideal medium through which to communicate with your patients and prospects.

Being heard above the noise is one of the biggest stumbling blocks for doctors, entrepreneurs and growing businesses. It's why most start-ups fail; it is why even more never get beyond "a good idea" scratched on a napkin.

Communication is typically the crucial link between vision and execution. **Unless you can communicate your vision to your investors, your employees, and most importantly, to yourself, your practice, no matter how inspired, will never succeed as it could.**

While there are many components of effective communication, dentists should begin with the most critical, **the message**. You must take your vision and translate it into a clear, focused and compelling message that can be conveyed to all. A book is the *best* medium to do this.

What are you going to say to your patients, team members, and prospective patients while you have their undivided attention?

21 Ways

Share Your Message with the World Through a Book

By Adam Witty

Share Your Message with the World Through a Book

BY ADAM WITTY

Let's face it, **the right book, in the right person's hands, at the right time, can change that person's life forever.** A book can pull someone out of debt, save a marriage, or mend a relationship between parent and child. It could very well change the life of your reader. How many people understand the huge effects their oral health and smile have on the length and quality of their lives, overall health, and longevity? Too few.

People write to communicate ideas and emotions, to challenge and motivate people into action, to reinforce beliefs or deconstruct perceptions. People read for enjoyment, self-enlightenment, and education...the list goes on. **Whatever** your message may be, there are people eager to read it.

Many doctors and business professionals reach a point in their career when they turn from success to significance. We all have an altruistic sense and desire to give back and contribute to the well-being of our fellow man. Many of us have a higher calling. **We have a message to share. A book is a vehicle to do all of the above.**

I want to share with you the story of Advantage author David Johnson. By sharing his message through a book, David went from being an amateur photographer to a national spokesperson and advocate for Sudanese people with his book, *Voices of Sudan.*

Books are the most powerful educational tools in the world, and they have enabled people to share stories, passion and knowledge that otherwise would not have been possible. There's a book with a message inside everyone. What's yours?

Even beyond your dental practice, do you have a charity, cause, or worthy organization that you want to support and draw attention to? A book is the perfect tool to do just that.

CHAPTER 12

Build Employee Loyalty and Create an Employee Training Guide with a Book

BY MICHAEL HUH

Build Employee Loyalty and Create an Employee Training Guide with a Book

By Michael Huh

How much time have you spent training and educating employees? How much time have you spent hiring new people to replace employees who left your company? Consider your hourly rate. How much money have you wasted to train and then retrain a revolving door of new people? Is this the best use of your time?

Smart CEOs, entrepreneurs and doctors have multiple uses for their books. But the really smart ones also use their books as educational tools for their employees, to train, educate, and build loyalty. What better way to build your team with your values than through your book?

Many great practices are driven by a strong team-focused core architecture or company culture. Another characteristic of these great practices is they have well-trained and educated employees. The amount of time, energy and money that is invested in training and education shows an employee that he/she is an asset of the practice, worthy of investing in. **Do your employees know your practice's vision, goals and strategies? A book is a terrific vehicle for educating your team while creating glue between employee and practice.**

Rather than reciting your vision to each employee, how about putting it in a book? Loyal team members create loyal patients.

Organizations and practices that work to create a partnership relationship with their employees significantly improve their service to patients and customers. Use a book to solidify this relationship.

HOW TO INFLUENCE AND MOVE PEOPLE WITHOUT TRYING: WHY PUBLISHING A BOOK PROVIDED UNEXPECTED BENEFITS FOR THIS NEW YORK DENTIST

When Dr. Michael Goldberg decided to write his book, he did it for a reason that differed from most authors. His book, *What the Tooth Fairy Didn't Tell You: The Wise Consumer's Guide to Dentistry in the Big Apple,* came to be because, as he said, "I got angry." After helping yet another patient who had received poor dental care, he wanted to share information on proper procedures as a "public service."

"I needed to do something to help people avoid that kind of problem—to avoid, as we call it, 'patch-up' dentistry. People are living longer and they are keeping their teeth. They need to know how to care for them better, and they need to figure out how they're being cared for, and whether it's a problem, or not."

And while his goal may have stemmed from anger, publishing his book provided this New York City dentist with benefits he didn't expect.

For one, he is enjoying stronger patient relationships due to new opportunities for education. His book is especially important, he has found, for "people who come in with problems they're unaware of or with problems they don't know how to deal with."

In addition to being a solid "educational tool," Dr. Goldberg also believes his book provides comfort and builds trust, especially with new patients. This is likely the result of the increased credibility enjoyed by authors, although he wasn't really looking for this outcome.

"I was a professor at Columbia for 30 years, and I also treat a lot of professionals. So, I have a lot of credibility. But there's no question that being an author and having a physical book that you've written makes you more credible."

And Dr. Goldberg experienced another interesting benefit after becoming a published author.

AN UNEXPECTED WAY TO INCREASE STAFF
LOYALTY AND NEW OPPORTUNITIES

After giving a copy to each of his staff members, Dr. Goldberg now provides his book to new hires as well. "It's almost a training manual. It gives them an idea of the language we use on a regular basis." This led to another, unanticipated bonus. "I've seen a difference in the staff. I think once they saw that I had published a book, they were a little more impressed. And that filters down to the patients."

His book has proven to be an easy way to impress and influence his staff even though it wasn't his original goal. Yet, the unforeseen benefits don't end here.

Dr. Goldberg has also used his book to raise money for a charity close to his heart. "I'm actually the president of an organization that helps fund a free children's dental clinic in Jerusalem. So, I ran a promotion through my practice. Anyone who wanted a book got one for a $20 donation. And all proceeds went to help my charity."

Overall, he has found that publishing his book has been a very "interesting experience" and now, he is "hooked" on writing.

"Now, I'm writing blogs and a column for a diabetes magazine. My credibility (as an author) has increased significantly, so I'm getting requests from people to write things. I've actually started to turn people down because I just don't have the time."

This is why he advises anyone considering a book to not hesitate. "If people like what you say and the way you say it, a book opens up other opportunities."

If you're hesitating about writing a book, why not talk with Advantage Media Group today? We can provide advice and give you ideas on how to use a book for your practice. We'll also tell you about an easy way to write your book, simply by talking your way through an outline that we help you develop.

Contact Advantage Media Group today for your free consultation by visiting advantagefamily.com/dental or calling 1.866.775.1696.

21 Ways

Create a Tipping Point and Compete Against Industry Giants with a Book

By Adam Witty

Create a Tipping Point and Compete Against Industry Giants with a Book

BY ADAM WITTY

If you were in the software business, you would probably know that Bill Gates of Microsoft has written a book. If you were in the restaurant business, you would probably know that Ray Kroc of McDonalds, Howard Schultz of Starbucks, and dozens of other restaurant entrepreneurs have written books. In fact, **many successful entrepreneurs and CEOs who are at the top of their industry have published books**.

Since most dentists do not have books, you can soar to the top by having one.

Not only can a book position you as a "giant," but if the book hits critical mass, it can create a dramatic tipping point for your business, even locally.

Writing a book can help you go global. After releasing your book to the world, you have the ability to reach out and touch people across the globe. Your patients may live in your neighborhood or across the world. **A book solidifies your success locally and extends your reach to broad, new areas you could have never gone without a book.**

CHAPTER 14

A Book Is a Virtual Sales Force

Increase Sales without Salespeople

By Michael Huh

A Book Is a Virtual Sales Force

Increase Sales without Salespeople

By Michael Huh

As a dental professional, you know that there are three ways to grow your business. First, acquire more patients. Second, do more business with the patients you already have. Third, do more work more frequently with the ones you have. To do any and all of these requires human energy in most cases.

The fundamental flaw with human energy (staff) is that they are expensive and have massive needs. When you increase your staff count, you proportionally increase your overhead, headaches and challenges. After all, people are people.

That said, **would you be interested in a proven way to increase your productivity without adding staff?** Allow me to introduce you to your virtual persuasion force: **your book**.

Your book allows you to be in multiple places at the same time (multiplicity), something we discussed in a previous chapter. It allows you to have a personal conversation with many people at the same time.

When patients, or prospects, read your book, they are focused solely on you, making it far easier to book the appointment. Savvy authors will also include direct response techniques, bounce-backs, and special offers within their book to keep the phone ringing and the new patient pipeline full.

A book is a cost-effective, direct-response marketing tool that, if used properly, will turn on the spigot of new leads, helping you increase your sales without adding overhead and staff. Best of all, books don't take two-hour lunches, make excuses or talk back!

21
Ways

Be Recognized and Remembered with a Book

By Adam Witty

Be Recognized and Remembered with a Book

BY ADAM WITTY

Only through a book can you record your thoughts, experiences, and history for your family, loved ones, and employees.

Have you considered how you will be remembered when your ticker stops ticking? I know, I know. This is a morbid question. Please forgive me. It is however, an important question. **What legacy will you leave behind?**

Will you be remembered for the positive impact you made on the people in your practice? Will you be remembered for the positive deeds you did on behalf of your community? How will your grandchildren or great grandchildren know you? If you are the founder of a practice and intend to have it outlive you, how will team members learn about the early years? How will they appreciate the core values and fundamentals on which you built the business? Those core values are essential to the long-term success of a practice and its people.

Maybe you'll be remembered for going viral. Just like a movie or hit song, books can go viral and can forever change the world. Take *Chicken Soup for the Soul* or *The Purpose Driven Life* as examples. Both books have made a huge impression on the world for their captivating yet simplistic messages. If they can do it, so can you!

Finally, recognition can be as simple as stroking one's ego. Every human has an ego, whether we are big enough to admit it or not. We all express our egos in different ways. For some, it is authoring a book.

BEYOND EXPERT STATUS AND INCREASED INCOME:
HOW A BOOK EXCEEDED EXPECTATIONS AND CREATED
NEW OPPORTUNITIES FOR THIS UK DENTIST

When Dr. Richard Guyver published his book in May 2013, he wanted to establish himself as an expert on the subject of the connection between dental health and overall well-being. Yet, in a few short months after publishing, he is getting far more opportunities, due to his book.

"The book is about how the mouth can impact general health in both positive and negative ways. A lot of people don't know this. So I wanted to raise the profile of that philosophy of dental care. And from a personal point of view, I wanted to establish my position as an expert in that area."

Dr. Guyver met these expectations in just five months after publishing. Media coverage and free publicity came almost immediately. "I've had the book in local press and national press in the UK. I've also had it mentioned on BBC TV. It's been very positive."

Along with this media coverage came one of his first unexpected opportunities. A local paper asked him to write a regular column for its online edition. And these articles are relatively quick to write since he uses his book as their foundation. As he says, "This would have been less likely to happen had I not had the book."

Yet, media attention was only step one. Dr. Guyver also gave copies of his book to patients. In addition to receiving compliments, he discovered that many found his book to be eye opening.

"Patients have said that it is written in a really nice, understandable way aimed at human beings rather than dentists or people with a lot of education. And a lot of them have said, 'I didn't realize how important the mouth was on general health.'"

With this positive feedback, Dr. Guyver saw another opportunity to increase patient referrals with his book. So, at the time of writing this book, he had sent three copies to each patient on his list. "I wanted them to have three books each: one for themselves and two to give to friends, neighbors, colleagues, or family members." And if the past successes of authors who made similar efforts are any indication, he will drum up new referrals.

While he waits for results from this campaign, Dr. Guyver has already seen an increase in new patients. "There certainly have been a few new patients who've come in, either directly or indirectly as a result of my book."

AND THIS RESPONSE WAS FOLLOWED BY ANOTHER SURPRISE . . .

In addition to drawing in new patients, Dr. Guyver has also attracted the attention of fellow dentists. "Some members of my profession have contacted me as a result of the book because they want to use the same philosophy in their practice."

This has led him to the idea of establishing a coaching group, another unforeseen spinoff benefit of his book. But he isn't stopping with this idea. He is now considering the possibility of coauthoring books with other dentists.

"I have an idea to help other noncompetitive dentists use the book to market their practice. There are blank pages at the front of the book, so we can profile them and how they use the philosophy as well. It will still be my book, but they can use it for their practice. The dentists could buy a bulk number of books, or alternatively, pay me to do it for them."

Given that similar strategies are used by other professionals, including Dr. Charles Martin, Dr. Guyver has a great opportunity to turn this idea into new revenue over the long run.

IMMEDIATE RESULTS LEAD TO INCREASED INCOME

It only took about five months after publishing for Dr. Guyver to see positive change in his practice. One of the most beneficial is the effect on his relationships with patients. "It's hard to attach a value, but I think it's quite important. A book gives you something to talk about with your patients. It gives patients something of interest, something new. So, I think that's quite important since I'm in a relationship-building business."

In addition, he has noticed that the book encourages patients to move forward with recommended procedures. "Some patients have taken up treatment which they were otherwise resistant to, which is good."

Plus, his book has attracted new patients in the short period of time after publishing. He is on track to increase his income as a result.

This is why he advises any professional who is sitting on the fence to get started.

"Just set some time aside to do it. And don't let other things impinge on that time. Don't wait until you have time, because you'll never get it done. It's all about saying, 'On Monday morning, I've got two hours I'm going to spend on my book, and nothing interrupts.'"

And this is exactly how he wrote his book, setting aside chunks of time to get his writing done.

"A lot of academic research has gone into my book. I read a number of scientific journals and essentially summarized them and wrote them in layman's terms so people can understand them. I probably wrote about a third of the book like that and then it was after that when I contacted Advantage. I got a number of suggestions from them on ways to improve it, to make it bigger, and more valuable."

This method clearly worked for Dr. Guyver, although if you're planning to write your manuscript, he says dictation software will speed up the process. As an alternative, he suggests that potential authors use our unique **Talk Your Book**™ program, which also makes book writing faster and easier.

Either way, he strongly believes the benefits are worth the effort. "It's worth doing even if you're not thinking about marketing your business because it's a sense of achievement to have done it, to get to the endpoint."

Whichever method you choose to produce your book, Advantage Media Group can help you become a published author. You can use our **Talk Your Book**™ program, or get our help with your manuscript, just as we did for Dr. Guyver. In either case, the end result will be a book that you can use to build your practice or business—and your income. Contact us today for your free consultation at advantagefamily.com/dental or by calling 1.866.775.1696.

A Book Is the Ultimate Networking Tool

By Michael Huh

A Book Is the Ultimate Networking Tool

By Michael Huh

Networking is an essential skill for most business professionals, but especially for doctors, entrepreneurs, Business owners, and CEOs.

There's a strong association between the doctor as a person and his or her practice demands. It is vitally important that doctors get out into the world and create and maintain relationships.

As Henry Ford once said, "Take away all of my money and leave me only my rolodex and in one year's time I will be a multimillionaire all over again." I suppose this illustrates the power of networking, or as the old saying goes, "It's not what you know; it's *who* you know."

I know what you're saying: *networking takes time and I don't have the time!* A book helps you network with all the people you want without taking too much time.

Wouldn't you like to have a book that would do the heavy lifting for you and connect your practice with other people, organizations and spheres of influence?

Let me tell you about Advantage author Bryan Crabtree. Bryan coauthored a book titled *The Advantage of Real Estate.* Bryan wrote the book with 11 other prominent real estate investors throughout the country. As a result of the book, Bryan has networked with another investor with whom he recently purchased a property. These two investors have a three-year plan to turn around the property and flip it for a very healthy profit. That one deal alone represents thousands of dollars for Bryan's bank account. That one deal alone was made possible by the networking generated from Bryan's book.

21 Ways

A Book Is the Ultimate Business Card

By Adam Witty

A Book Is the Ultimate Business Card

BY ADAM WITTY

Typically, in business, when you meet with a client, what is the first thing you do when you sit down with that individual? You slide your business card across the table, right? I want you to start thinking about your book as your business card.

Say something in the nature of *"Mr. Prospective Patient, thank you so much for spending a few minutes with me today. As a small token of my appreciation, I would like for you to have a copy of my latest book, just published by Advantage Media Group. I think you will really enjoy the book."*

Now, let us address the obvious. As soon as those words flow from your mouth and the book moves from you to the prospective patient, two BIG things happen.

First, the prospect will immediately straighten up in his chair and take great interest in everything that you have to say. Whereas initially the prospect may have viewed his time with you as an expected part of the visit, **as an author, you immediately go from busy doctor who barely has enough time for me to an esteemed expert who cared enough to give me a copy of his book.**

Second, your prospect is now "pre-sold" on you before you even open your mouth. The reason is simple: **your book is the ultimate sales letter or brochure and sells the prospect on why you're THE authority on your particular subject.** Rather than asking the typical question of "What is the fee?" the prospect will move to questions such as "Would you consider taking me on as a patient?"

It is extremely important that you make sure one of the last pages of your book has ALL contact information for you and your practice. The contact page is the number-one, most important page in an entire 300-page book. Some might argue that the other 299 pages are irrelevant. The point is your book *is* your business card.

Rather than sliding a business card across the table, start sliding your book across the table instead. You will observe big changes immediately.

CHAPTER 18

21 Ways

Build Brand Recognition and Brand Equity for Your Practice with a Book

By Michael Huh

Build Brand Recognition and Brand Equity for Your Practice with a Book

By Michael Huh

Have you ever heard of the Starbucks Coffee Company? Do you have a cup of Starbucks in your hand right now while you are reading this book? In 1999 Starbucks Chairman and CEO Howard Schultz wrote a book titled *Pour Your Heart into It: How Starbucks Built a Company One Cup at a Time.*

Do you think the CEO of Starbucks wrote his book as a networking tool or as a business card? Maybe neither. But **Howard Schultz did write the book to create goodwill for the Starbucks brand and drive new people into Starbucks stores.** In 1999, when the book was published, Starbucks had

2,500 store locations. In 2008 Starbucks had over 17,000 store locations.

How can you leverage a book to build brand recognition and brand equity for your practice or organization?

21 Ways

Build Your List

Use a Book for Lead Acquisition

By Adam Witty

Build Your List

Use a Book for Lead Acquisition

BY ADAM WITTY

Many years back, my friend, colleague and Advantage author Tom Antion and I were having a conversation about Internet marketing when he asked me a question that has forever changed my life.

The question was "*What is your computer?*" When I stared dazed and confused at him, he blurted out, "*Your computer is an ATM in which you can instantly print money whenever you need it.*"

Tom's point was that by building a large list of prospects and customers, savvy marketers are able to mail to them at any time and generate instant response, which translates to instant sales. In fact, Tom's list of 110,000 customers, prospects and subscribers generates between $90,000 to $200,000 per month.

My point is simple: **you should be using a book to generate subscribers to your list.** These subscribers are prospective patients and existing patients. You should have numerous references contained within your book directing them to a free report, article, teleseminar, or something else of value. You want them to "raise their hand" and say, "YES, I want to hear from you. I want to learn from you. I want you to stay in contact with me."

Another master practitioner of this art is marketing guru and Advantage author Dan Kennedy, known to many as the godfather of direct response marketing and the millionaire maker. Dan subtly weaves free resources (aka offers to join his "list") throughout his book.

Take a page from us, Dan Kennedy and Tom Antion's books (no pun intended) and **use a book to drive subscribers to your list.**

This is an entirely new concept for most doctors and it is power packed with the ability to change your marketing and new-patient acquisition forever.

21 Ways

Use a Book to Become a Local Celebrity and Speaker

By Michael Huh

Use a Book to Become a Local Celebrity and Speaker

By Michael Huh

A book can do wonders for speakers in increasing their number of gigs and celebrity status where they live. **Speaking is the best way to promote and sell your book locally and influence members of the public to become your patients.** Being an author and speaker go hand in hand like peas and carrots or burgers and fries.

Meeting planners and event chairs, who are responsible for booking a majority of all speakers, LOVE authors. Many meeting planners won't consider a speaker who has not earned the "good housekeeping seal of approval," a published book.

If you ever decide to use public seminars to promote your practice, (which you should do and we can show you how) your book is the ideal tool to give to attendees. Some will devour it right away and then become your patients. Others will delay reading but still become patients because "you wrote the book." Others will put the book aside until they have a problem and then use the book to contact you by phone or online. Still others will pass the book along to friends and neighbors. **Unlike brochures, books are things people keep**. It just seems like too much of a loss to throw a book away, wouldn't you agree?

How to Dissolve Fee Sensitivity with Your Book

By Adam Witty

How to Dissolve Fee Sensitivity with Your Book

BY ADAM WITTY

As a dentist, your book for patients elevates you above everyone else. To most, you become the "specialist," the "esteemed expert."

With this new status comes certain rights and expectations.

You, as the doctor, have the right to charge more. Patients expect it. After all, you are the expert. Moreover, your book is the tool to lift you above the concept that a dentist is a dentist is a dentist. Your book grants you authority and status, which brings you the right to set up the rules of engagement with your patients.

One doctor I know has completely changed the character of his practice because of his books. His clientele went from local only—as he often struggled to get the new patients he wanted—to national and international as a result of writing his books.

The same thing has happened to Advantage author, Dr. Charles Martin. On any one day, his schedule of patients will come from all parts of the state and sometimes other states, even foreign countries. You see, he is a living example of the power of books. May I suggest that you can be too? Get a book published.

With the Advantage team, we can make the entire process not only easy but fun and fast. Isn't it time to get your due, to change the way you practice to one of your choosing? Contact us today at advantagefamily.com/dental or 1.866.775.1696.

How to Write a Book— Quickly and Easily—On a Dentist's Schedule

You Can Be a Published Author Even if
You're Not a "Born Writer"

By Michael Huh

How to Write a Book— Quickly and Easily—On a Dentist's Schedule

You Can Be a Published Author Even if You're Not a "Born Writer"

By Michael Huh

This book has pointed out advantages and benefits of having your own book as a dentist. It is an extensive list, wouldn't you agree?

So what's stopping you?

Let's think logically about this for a moment. What is your goal in having a book as a dentist? To gain the advantage of prestige, influence, notoriety and patients begging you to be their dentist, right? To create a marketing advantage that puts you at the top of the hill among your peers, wouldn't you agree?

You don't need to be famous nationwide. You only need to be famous where you live, where your patients live. We call this being slightly famous. (Sure, you *will* get more famous in your region and the Internet does help, but still, you want your gains to be where you live, where your patients and prospective patients live).

The problems of traditional publishing are most likely to prevent you from ever getting a book published at all.

Traditional publishers outright reject 90–95 percent of all the book manuscripts they receive. Left to your own devices, you are highly likely to be a part of this group of rejects. Who wants a 1 in 20 chance to get a book published after spending hundreds of hours of valuable time getting it ready? Frankly, dentistry just isn't a topic on the mind of the general public. (But *it is* for your patients and prospective patients).

There are a host of other problems with traditional publishing. Over 200,000 books are published every year. The average book run is 5,000 copies—*total*. For most authors, after a couple of hundred are sold, the rest sit gathering dust in a garage or storage facility.

Fact: traditional publishers are lousy at marketing books, except when it comes to the already successful authors. They concentrate their marketing and distribution efforts on the top 20 percent of their authors. As a new author, your chances of getting that kind of help are nil.

Here is a whole list of other problems with traditional publishing:

- Loss of creative control: the manuscript you slaved over could be radically altered by a traditional publisher to make it more marketable.

- Poor marketing support: they expect you to create your audience.

- For every traditionally published book that does make it through the publishing gauntlet, only one in 15 succeeds in the marketplace.

This leaves the odds of success at incredibly low levels.

Let's do the math.

Five percent of submissions are accepted: 25 out of 1,000 (the other 95 percent fail).

Seven percent of accepted books succeed once they make it to the marketplace (93 percent fail). So what are the odds exactly?

Seven percent of 25 in 1,000 = **less than two authors out of 1000 actually "make it" in traditional publishing!**

Can we agree those aren't good odds?

You have too much to do to play *that* losing game. Wouldn't you agree?

There is a better way. But before we talk about that, what about self-publishing? Doesn't that eliminate that traditional publishing failure rate? Not so fast.

Of course, self-publishing is an alternative. Some Advantage authors have done this before, but I can promise you, they won't make that mistake again.

So what are the problems with self-publishing?

1. Time: You still have to spend a lot of your time producing the writing. This can amount to hundreds of hours—even thousands of hours. It is not uncommon for writers to take one to two years to produce a book, writing full-time! Even after you write the book, it takes time to get it published after you have written the whole thing, typically 9–24 months!

2. Money: What is your time worth? What is the real cost of producing a book on your own? Even at a mere $100 hourly rate, this alone could total $20,000–$50,000 in your time just for getting it written, not including the other necessary parts of getting a book self-published.

3. Editing: Even after all that time, effort and energy, you'll need an editor to convert your book into a more readable form. Many authors are very finicky about what editors do. Bet you certainly wouldn't be bothered by an editor's knife cutting out the inside of your manuscript created during your nights and weekends, which meant sacrificing personal and family time—right? The answer is

self-evident. No one likes it. Moreover, there is the back and forth of drafts that can seem endless.

4. Professionalism: Few self-published works really look professional. Remember the purpose of your book is to establish your professionalism and your position as an expert and the "go-to guy" where you live. Book design, covers and layout matter—a lot. Are you capable of doing it yourself? (It's enough to make you forget why you wanted a book in the first place!) Look! What would you say to a patient who tried to do his/her own dentistry? I think you get the point.

5. Distribution: A book needs distribution channels. As a self-publisher, you are responsible for these. Do you know how to get your book on Amazon or Barnes & Noble? Who wants to store the books and then, one-by-one, sell them by phone or online? Who has the people available to do that?

6. Frustration: All of these concerns add up and drain your enthusiasm for your "baby," your book. Getting a book published is a lot of work, time, money and effort, even as a self-publisher. Your book will never be a best seller. That's not its purpose. Its purpose is to give you prestige, position as the expert and the power to practice the way you want, right where you live. You could work like crazy on your book only to have it fail.

7. Ability to write: I haven't mentioned this one yet, but it could be one of the most important reasons to avoid both traditional and self-publishing routes. Most professionals are strong in science and math. English and writing were soft skills you may have never appreciated or done well. Then there is the matter of understanding how to put together a book in the first place. How long should it be? What "voice" should it express? How should the words and parts be arranged for maximum impact?

Given all these problems, it is pretty easy to say that both traditional and self-publishing models are just about impossible for you as a dental professional. Wouldn't you agree?

That's why you have an *immense* opportunity.

So few dentists have books that *your* book can be **the competitive edge** when it comes to prospective patients choosing a dentist.

Here is another thought: With a book, you give your current patients bragging rights: "My dentist is Dr._____. He wrote this book on dentistry here in _____." How much more likely are they to refer to you and remain loyal to you? Just know this: a lot!

By now you have probably figured out that I have been leading you up to this point: "How can I get all the advantages of my own book without all the pain?"

ARE YOU READY TO ACHIEVE MORE THAN
YOU EVER THOUGHT POSSIBLE?

A book is your game changer. It's the missing link you need to accelerate your practice, communicate your message, and reach your dreams.

Success from your book begins with a strong strategy, develops with experienced editing, grows with sound marketing, and takes flight with a monetization plan. At Advantage, we can help you with one or all of these steps, depending on where you are in the process. You'll be an author with a professionally published book that imparts *your* message to your audience.

ARE YOU TAKING THE FIRST STEP? NOT SURE WHERE TO BEGIN?

With our ***Fast Start Author Program***, we'll help you develop your book strategy and editorial outline. You'll walk away with a blueprint unique to you and your business. From here, you decide on your next step, whether it's publishing with us or creating it on your own. Whatever you decide, the insight you will glean from this process will be invaluable to you even if you *never* write a book.

DO YOU SEE A BOOK IN YOUR FUTURE BUT WORRY ABOUT THE TIME IT WILL TAKE TO WRITE IT?

Create your book in less than a day with our *Talk Your Book® creation system*. You simply speak your ideas following an outline that we create for you. Our editorial team puts your ideas on paper. You review, revise, and finally, approve your manuscript. We help you add the finishing touches, and you become a published author in just a few months!

ARE YOU READY TO PUBLISH YOUR MANUSCRIPT?

If you have a manuscript, even *partly* finished, our seasoned team will edit and polish your book with your guidance and input. We use your ideas to create a professional cover design, inviting cover copy, and custom graphics or illustrations for your book's interior. Finally, with our *Launch Your Book® publishing system* we'll distribute your book to more than 25,000 bookstores and online retailers. Your life will be forever changed from this point on!

HAVE YOU INVESTED IN A BOOK BUT HAVEN'T THOUGHT ABOUT HOW TO KEEP THE MARKETING MOMENTUM GOING?

Our done-for-you *Book The Business™ marketing services* give you the tools you need to make your book a success. You simply provide us with your book or other content, and we provide the marketing tools and support. Then, watch your presence grow with ongoing marketing, speaking opportunities, and publicity.

IS IT TIME TO MAKE MORE MONEY FROM YOUR BOOK?

With our *Monetize Your Book® online learning system*, we help you convert your book or speeches into engaging, self-paced online courses for you to sell on your website. We work with you to develop a course structure, tape your presentation in our professional studio, and monetize your course online. Before you know it, you'll be making money while you sleep.

WITH OUR HELP, IN A FEW SHORT MONTHS, YOU CAN JOIN THE RANKS OF PUBLISHED AUTHORS.

You can add this title to your biography, website, and business card. You can enjoy the benefits a book provides—from new opportunities and increased income, to free publicity and celebrity status—as hundreds of Advantage authors have.

Or, you can maintain the status quo.

The choice is yours. So why not contact us at advantagefamily.com/dental, or by phone at 1.866.775.1696, and tell us how we can help you best?

Your new opportunities begin with *this* first step.

REGISTER
YOUR BOOK

AND ACCESS FREE RESOURCES FOR POTENTIAL AUTHORS!

It doesn't matter where you are in the world, Adam can help you share your Stories, Passion, and Knowledge with the world in the form of a published book.

Visit BUILDYOURDENTALPRACTICE.COM/REGISTER to access these free resources:

 RECEIVE a subscription to the Author Success University™ monthly teleseminar wherein successful authors and book marketing experts reveal their tips and tricks for marketing and growing a business with a book

 REGISTER for a webinar led by Adam Witty: "How to Quickly Write, Publish, And Profit From A Book That Will Grow Your Business"

 **COMPLETE** Advantage's Publishing Questionnaire and receive a complimentary Discovery Call with an acquisitions editor to help you determine if your ideas, concepts, or manuscript are worth turning into a book

ACCESS ALL OF THE ABOVE FREE RESOURCES BY REGISTERING YOUR BOOK AT

BUILDYOURDENTALPRACTICE.COM/REGISTER